POEMS 2000-2005

POEMS 2000-2005

Hugh Maxton

Carysfort Press

A Carysfort Press Book in association with Peter Lang

POEMS 2000-2005
by Hugh Maxton

First published in Ireland in 2005 as a paperback original by Carysfort Press, 58 Woodfield, Scholarstown Road, Dublin 16, Ireland

ISBN 978-1-78997-048-7

© 2005 Copyright remains with the author

Typeset by Carysfort Press
Cover design by Alan Bennis

The publication of this work was supported by an Arts Council Grant

Caution: All rights reserved. No part of this book may be printed or reproduced or utilized in any form or by any electronic, mechanical, or other means, now known or hereafter invented including photocopying and recording, or in any information storage or retrieval system, without permission in writing from the publishers.

Do you remember, Lord Gregory, that night at Cappoquin,
When we both changed pocket handkerchiefs and that
 against my will?
Yours was pure linen, Love, and mine was coarse cloth;
Yours cost one guinea, Love, and mine but one groat.

Do you remember, Lord Gregory, that night at Cappoquin,
When we both changed rings of our fingers and that
against my will?
Yours was pure silver, Love, and mine was blocked tin;
Yours cost one guinea, Love, and mine but one cent.
    (Old Ballad)

Do you ever remember a European question on which Ireland did not at once take the opposite side to England? Well that kills all thought & encourages the most miserable kind of mob rhetoric.
    (W. B. Yeats to George Russell, May 1919)

Some of these poems first appeared in *Cyphers*, *The Honest Ulsterman*, *Stand*; and Evelyn Conlon (ed.) *Later On: The Monaghan Bombing Memorial Anthology* (2004).

'No Sign Given to It' and 'Clonallis, Late Summer' were first published in hOMAGHe, a limited edition (with drawings by Margaret Fitzgibbon) privately published in 2004 by Bamberg Press and printed at the Print Studio, Cambridge.

Permission to re-publish these items is gratefully acknowledged.

Contents

Adam in Paradise: Quartet
    i   Renunciation
    ii   Dedication Later
    iii   Deadlock
    iv   960

PLANTED   5

Mersea Island
Questions for John Prine
Winter Solstice
Broken Long Measure
To the Memory of Lily Webster
Dry Lightning
Pellet
Moregrove
Dead Habitat
Uncle Peter's Purgatory
The Shuck
Herbal for Anna Hartnett
Legend of the Lamp Room

THE TROUBLED   **33**

Shelling Hill
Sermon on the Mountjoy Side-Step
Incident in the Life of Michael Davitt
Pellets of Stanza and Prose
No Sign Given to It
Clonallis, Late Summer
Nutting
The Broken Stile
Pomona

IXION'S WHEEL   **57**

Near Sizewell Beach
Not Yacht-Club
Eurydice
Rhymes for Eurydice
The Gardens Quartet
Up and Under
Allotments

LAST THING   **75**

Numbers for Josh and Abigail Cohen
Miserere
For Bice Portinari, For Example
Matin
Salt and Light
One Animal's Return
Nearby Drung, County Cavan
The Enlightened Cave
Colophon

ADAM IN PARADISE: QUARTET

i   RENUNCIATION

Stormy blast
Nor home.
Normative cabin.

Then text at midnight
Terse as verse
Namelessly known.

A tide calm to the point
Only hidden dangers
Are visible to us

Visible to me
To the other
Who makes up us.

Ask a sign, ask it
Either in the depth?
I will not ask.

If we look long
Enough in our
Directions the distance

Is constant
As desire for
The narrow water.

Make me in thy likelihood

ii   DEDICATION LATER

The river is no distance
And birds without number.
The viewing balcony of this cabin
Looks into it.

I have locked my self in tonight
By a twist of the hand
With a key that ticks still
On its empty picture-hook.

Then there is you, absorbed
As Nature her self.
When we touch it is to give
The impression we carry

Some thing between us,
A stone or panel perhaps
From which the word hope
Has been cut with careful letters.

iii   DEAD LOCK

In snarls and funeral orations
To speak of civic earth
In a closed lane
Beyond Newbliss.

Wind drops, the lake
Lies to perfection
On the reflected skies,
Before the hills in order.

It might be so
From generations.
But the memory
Of what we forgot.

iv   960

Where I might lay down my self
after impromptus of God.
You, for example, unique,
the one but not only, cite
things yet to be said aloud

yet heard from afar in this
unyet composed or psalmic
preparation of what has.
Mention it, leave the word be,
returning ghost of pureness.

planted

MERSEA ISLAND

The pheasant in Mrs Dence's garden
Has two wives not fallen to the gun.

Three birds harass
Her worm-rich acre of grass.

QUESTIONS FOR JOHN PRINE

Will the country dry out,
The great black tear you spoke about
Drop finally from sight?

You no more take notice
Than I renounce
My soggy benefice.

The river flows one way only,
Tiber or Moy;
What blood carries the moly?

Have you a clue
How charms work on radio?
Has the rain fallen anyhow?

Or is it popcorn
In liquid form
From the unsold farm?

The different wring each other's fingers
Below table, neither singers
Nor jury, just listeners.

Will the viscous give up?
Will the music decompose
Into vice and syrup?

And then the ultimate teaser:
What of worshipful Caesar,
And the missing tears?

WINTER SOLSTICE

At sundry times of dead growth God needs stroll
Behind the book of our making to preen
Her moustache and by other means pluck hay
Out of season, while the poulterer's knife

Works indifferently among fair and foul.
What generations, Godfrey asked, must we
Lodge in the bonny banks of clay
Till the welcome's more than Get a Life?

Light dies early and often. From a hole
In his occupied universe, the mean
Of angels and devils calls in dismay
For a truce, one glance at her rump, new strife.

BROKEN LONG MEASURE

> *We went along the fence and came to the garden fence, where our shadows were.*
> — William Faulkner (1897-1962)

1

My quarter-acre wilderness
Contains one hell, a bower of bliss,
A blackened hearth, puddles of ice,
The rusted nib of Abram's knife.
Here I thrive without a wife,
Mending fences, herding mice.

Ditches open to disgorge
Buckled wheel and unmade bed,
Trophies from a buried forge,
Springs to prove a maidenhead
Ceded in a previous
Unspotted delving in our source.

Scanning pictels on the screen
I find my forbear's tenement
Of clay (York Street, No. 19)
Retreated by a century
Through grey steel doors, the rebuilt slum
Of Dublin's New Jerusalem.

Reticence like his I'd own
With shallow wit for alibi.
Gradually, it seems, I'm known
To be in truth unknowable.
I rusticate in Claraghy
No *vox clamans*, neighbourly, dull.

The mail van brings its daily load,
Bills and flyers, the holy junk
Of tin-pot chapel: so abound
Hostilities of here and nunc.
I practice as a wayward monk,
Apostate in the lost & found.

2

Mercury palms Goodman Tommy
Secrets due beyond Cootehill.
I'd model souls on his bonhomie,
And tell my own to bide its time
Or hide facetiously in mime.
Let the word spring as it will:

Cleft of rock or urbane Commie,
Whatever the clouds presage
The tedium is the message.
    – Oh innocent deliverer
Of round earth's fixed palaver,
The unmoved answer moves us still!

Transplanted twice I mind in turn
Growth about the haggard stook,
Hedge of beech spiked with blackthorn,
A variegated bush I hate,

Ancient fuchsia bleeding late,
Hazel, alder, sessile oak.

Calvin's angel writes to kiss
As though I were a soul remiss.
I scramble visits. Let her mull
On what has rooted hereabouts,
Double rows of name and doubt,
Rank nettle in the fuel house.

Days I fiddle with the rhymes
Counterplotting their upset,
Throwing in a bump of clay,
Fluffing lest it might display
Elegance or a learnèd scheme.
(I stumble for to keep my feet.)

Who runs may read no shining path;
The guttered book and pointed silence
Darken a damaged common sense.
Shadows thicken into wrath
At druid bunker, virtual rath –
Temples of the psychopath.

Just diversionary anger
Gratifies the rage for peace.
To shove aside the prefab hut
Improves the view of a neighbour's
Field. I abandon my jacket
Swinging on a plastic hanger.

With its steadying delays
Slow evening tempers dooms of fury.
The pink escallonia sprays
Scent the porch, rooted potpourri

For a moment rinses the mind.
All before the tree were kind.

Then news at six, its many truths
Unhinge the half-door, the tooth's
On edge, eyes drain out of pity.
Black ice gathers, samples explode.
The police re-collect three youths
Straight from God's roundabout road.

Offerings for the newshawk
Their blood clots on the hard shoulder.
Eternal foes renew peace talks,
Inch out the short lives. An older
Father stares back from the Middle East.
Medics declare the kids were pissed.

3

Author and maker of all things –
Altars, cradles, knives and swings -
Beseech me I beseech you; grace
The fatherhood without the blood,
Peculiar ground in every place,
Forgiveness in your looking-glass.

A fig for that. Next to nothing
Sits by the fireside and glowers
At the blank screen of his horrors,
Frailty dropped in fear and loathing,
Memory fixed on its own faulty
Bench, never knowing the hour.

Routine inspires a better end
Than ever agonizing earns.
Lunkish sincerity runs dry
Into its own vacuity.
'Who thinks in Latton?' I think
And rise from my private stink.

The carnal angel phones again,
My roof-tree is as right as rain,
We are a garden walled around
Though intimate as hart and hound.
A truce declared, we love alone
This shared yet interstellar zone.

At night I smoke a pipe and pace
The ten-foot margin of my shuck
To watch the moonlight light on muck
And yet divulge its pally face.
Guessing shadows, stems and trunks
I spot the dark trees as dawn breaks.

One sapling guards against the fence,
A smoke-blue cedar that foreknows
My sooner death. With little blows
The wind disperses violence
Among our limbs. No god of sense
Would think me worth a sacrifice.

TO THE MEMORY OF LILY WEBSTER

In a brief lay-by by the primrose highway
The House enjoyed your quiet rule,
The barn behind it gave room to echo
Each empty summer the handsome owl.

Then George and Albert conveyed a harvest,
The haggard rising to block the sun;
Now coaches park there, there is not dark there,
Macreddin roisters the dead and gone.

DRY LIGHTNING
      (Agnes Nemes Nagy, 1922-1991)

A dying haggard lamb
Hunted under
The embassy lamp

Of a third place.
Emblems everywhere
Long ago evacuated.

She spoke of the just truth
In a tongue without
Gender or guile.

Complaining with love
Of its too great tunefulness,
Darkling.

Lon dubh aonair
I Londuin
'Is an gealt ámharach

Far from the little leaves.
Of that dusty light
A handful still cleaves.

PELLET

And the scops owl
Thinks to itself.

MOREGROVE

Where water's neither hard nor soft
Nor the weather heard of,
We sat down and scoffed
The inhabitants – herds,
Tillers of soil, aye the soil itself.
    Wind soughs through an empty wood.
    How come the fox-gloves?

We bait deuteronomy,
Torture and taxonomy.
Dying, they let on.
Trying, we knew less and less
Of their unkindliness.
    Wind sighs through an empty wood.
    How come the fox-gloves?

We mind that time when brother
Made strange with brother
And yet confide the heather
From the hell for leather
In search of apple and oil.
    Wind sings through an empty wood.
    How come the fox-gloves?

Now, it's six of one. The loft
Brims both eaves of a plank
A long drop above beef flank.
Someone said the combine coughed
At the water fled uphill.
    Wind sounds through an empty wood.
    How come the fox-gloves?

DEAD HABITAT

degeneranti genus opprobrium

For Simon and Danielle

Calke Abbey's a must. On the kitchen formica
Two trout from the age of the flapper.
Below stairs, we are able to witness
A Great War cook splitting hares.
Ranked owls in the withdrawing-room remain
Hearing the Moscow news with howls.
Crewes jumped this ship of counterstatement,
The kids' room smelling what they dumped.

The rhymes don't matter, or fatten
In places reserved for a Latin motto.
We leave, my son and I, for the natural world
Of carparkland and mugtrees, hurled
Like our first parents from the ruined porch –
Abandon to a paradisal lurch
The maker of heavenly views from whence
To judge the silver and the buried fence.

That leaves the journey home, at most
An hour or two sins against the Holy Ghost.
The way is clear, the plantation fresh
On both sides, like consubstantial flesh
Committed to the trip, the grip, the trial
Of bad language proven in denial.
It takes longer than anyone believes in
To learn remission as a discipline.

One last thing. Through the wipers, he waves
To a towering stump gaunt in the pastured

Playground. Here hid no king of kings
(Or legend of that doom) in a tree died
Roughly in time with the youngest regicide.
Since it offers bats their henge, plays
Host to the humble-loving field-mouse,
Roost to ravens, and keeps the beetle housed.

So what's the trump? Cavaliers from Hollywood
Retake the formal garden, as the quickly dead
Change for the next delay. Formaldehyde
Bubbles to no effect in the studio
As peahens and Peter Rubens collapse in glue.
Forget the rain, the weather's parked outside.
A tree funnels upwards after death,
Wooden volcano, preemptive aftermath.

UNCLE PETER'S PURGATORY
for Warwick Gould and Deirdre Toomey

* Prologue to Fugue

A fireband marching, from Rathdrum-dar-um,
Crossed the stream of water. The Little
River held firm between banks of earth.
The weather was gorse orange through a mist
The loyal ewes marched through. The post
Burned like mountain ash, the latter postman
And his household standing by the roadside
Bags packed where the manufactory was.

All wethers put to the knife, the yeos dash-
Churning every sceachthorn for bolted Holt.
Murder by the national school, burial
By the graveyard, Martha and Muriel
Fled hereabouts from below to the south.
To be laid restfully in a field of brown ricks.
The same river flowed despite the dippers,
The same weather was coming to a close.

Was it Nature or History which rhymed
But rhymed with nothing? In recollection
The tune seems in order, inaudible.
Some of them bells, the bandsmen were all friends
Of each other. Or tocsins. Nobody
Knew the end of that line or any line,
The wanderer rehearsed among his pals
Still wedded to the moll he'd never meet.

A fifty-year-old reticent manager
Held me a moment for my sponsors.
I sometimes play with the idea that

The features of his face, suffering and
Tender, powerful and earnest, were shared out
Among two or three gathered together.
Soon without, I still do my composition,
Track Seadhna to the bottom of a page.

Snow in October, distant tram-strikes
And the coming rant, mohair on horseback
Or the pig's, buying principles on tick.
That's the timetable, the bellyband
Swaddling miners who trudge a Madman's Lane,
Hammers dulcimers black and blue the sky.
We stride on as if the racket were sound,
The names mere convenience, meaning music.

Music blown apart by the growing trees
Spins into the cupped hand, toxic fox-glove.
One August summer I put pipe to mouth,
Rekindled the tenor of my father.
It was my sole day of memmoration:
A lead letter fell from his epitaph
To grey chippins, a solid tear, bullet
Above his skull, among the wife's strangers.

* Oraid

by this sally
remember the reverend
who gave his life

his remains
she remains

* Now

Meltingly, Young Britart drops
Red body from his latest work.
Time and theme – why pronounce
A fallen difference?

Snow leaks to a three-point plug
As if this gazer gave a shrug;
Takes instead a long-term view
Of pushers in the headlong queue –

The bowsey and the catamount
Artists by their own account,
The boss and covey (with the fence
They leaned on for common sense)

Spittle-sot and connoisseur,
Drainpipe jockey, backpage whore.
Hand in liquid hand they panto
Their cute Ability Canto.

* Paidir

departing saints,
consider a former
wild protestant's
thoughts on the future:
no hell but this one.

* Mr Love's Baptismal Service (1947)

Trees move slowly
During the century

A minim, taper,
Flyleaf, end paper.

Only the dead seem
To be our children.

Antics in a burning hay
Spinning jenny on the lawn

Names and accidentals
Nearby in death

Jimmy and father
And Lily Webster.

Judgment of mice
Industry of worms,

Pomp and
Slurry-tanks.

* Now Resumed

The wounded bully soils his roost,
Humility his dying boast,
Terry Alt or Native Peeler,
Needful killjoy to a killer.

This Terry (caoining Irish Letters)
Is often seen to ape his fetters,
Pretend to what is actual,
And sing for brandy when in hell
Among the gratefully oppressed.
He serves the unconvicted best,
Laughingly lugubrious,
Exuding pleasure from his puss.

Beside him flies a handsome devil
Pole-vault champion on the level
Off the field, showing his mits
To any busman's face that fits.

A disappearance unbemoaned,
Their double act of derring-don't.

* Luke 9: 21-27

Then he shouted now, whoever he was.
He repeated now, but I was too late
To seize the perennial moment, ingrate
That I long was. So was I lost and saved

To exile in my small homes, one faithful love
Or another in constant attendance,
A good book in hand the inheritance
From Father's first wife's sister-in-law.

* [title deleted]

        imitate to accuse
        limit hate to refuse
        the rattle of those
        armament bangles.

        longing rests
        incorruptible yet
        amid ornis
        of the Dalty's

        underwood, the owl
        on the coffin all
        nighttime, bawl
        in atonality.

* Systematic Now

Dublin is a spiritual
Condition much like hell.

When spin's the soul's torment
Nothing's real or meant

And lost causes prey
On their own Saint Antony.

He is not on his own,
He is not on the town:

He's been Cerberus all along,
No devil but the devil's tongue.

Enraged to find the glass a blank
He knows to neither wink nor thank.

While increasing night invades
He spots a fellow dog in shades.

Statue-blind, his well-drilled eyes
Bottle up their wild surmise

Until the music never stops.
Sorrygoround of clever flops.

*– They had chained their throats
And had the throats of bards.*

* Nunc Dimittis

To die here is better
curtain   and
fanfare.

Stuff
enough.

THE SHUCK

Describes it,
A trench of water
No more moving
Nor the mills of God
It drove

Shallow enough
To reflect
My intellect
On the high sky
Above.

It has stood
The collapse of time
Into effect
Resumed
After the flood.

And how?
The Dutch
Landskip
At my feet's
Biblium pauperum

And a heron
Initials
The far margin
Like the unlike
Dove.

Or, docile as cattle
It has lain
Beside fields

Of early hay
And sour docken

Flowed beneath
A new garden's
Soiled border
Mild as dough,
Thorns white as flour.

HERBAL FOR ANNA HARTNETT

No one is ever ill on rue,
Though bone-breaking asphodel
Flitters the island air
With pungent innocence.

If no one is ever ill, we too
Brighten the lightless hotel
Adopting quite an air
Orphaned by reticence.

Drúchtín (or the round-leafed sundew)
Draws soiled breath by the starved well.
Bog rosemary is soft hair
Beautiful as your great aunt's.

Pulling the herb of grace, no shrew
Savours a meat he bites well,
Or the settled badger will fare
Among grubs and rabbit scents.

Nature's not lost but overdue
At the ports we travel:
You shall treasure its care
Beyond measure of rents.

LEGEND OF THE LAMP ROOM
for Finian, then aged six

When the hero
Stepped down here
In search of lively bait
For his *Soul of Man under Stairs*
Five brass bellies sat in wait
Like five Buddhas up from Lough Fee.

Their slim chimneys
Curved like salmon
Biting the hand-made fly.
Their mantles were muslin-
Snug in a time of Famine
As bugs in a lawyer's wig.

While he stood firm
Years tripped over.
The door tapped on the floor,
Glass melted and froze
In the nine-light windows,
Vacant, rasping for more.

The basement
Lay in amazement
While the lamps rattled
Blindly inside the casement,
A noise to impress
Less than heroes.

Songs died
From tongue to tongue.
Herons clattered outside

Dropping their pencil-cases
From ignorant pride,
Or snapping their gallusses.

Vikings
And submarines
Beat up the Little Killary.
Anger among the angler's things
Made a rod for his own back
As he bore the pillory.

Dog-days in the fox-holes
Desert-rats in Desertmartin,
So it was as he thought.
But nothing is certain
But you do it and know it
In the one swoop.

And the hero knew
What he must do,
Put herons to flight
Across the straits of water
Where the coarse fish finished
All that was left of light.

The lamp room lay still awake.
He reached past the tilly
To choose the unblinking storm
And go search for lug and worm,
To plummet the plum-dark lake –
While the Buddhas looked plain silly.

the troubled

SHELLING HILL, NEAR FAUGHART AND OTHER HISTORIC SITES

> *Last week I saw a woman flay'd,
> and you will hardly believe, how
> much it altered her Person for
> the worse.* (Jonathan Swift)

> *We hope the guards will soon put the
> family out of their misery.* (Sinn Féin)

Half a mile from last year's truth,
Police set up their plastic booth.
A hour of digging and they find
What time and gunmen left behind
These English-funded Famine walls –
A body lifted from the Falls.
Is this the former Jean McConville
Or Adam's progeny run vile?

Children dogging by the sea
Were for years the first to see
Her small remains in army issue,
A belt and with it body tissue,
A cardie less than fully blooded
And so an object to be studied.
'We hope,' the killers' kin declare,
'Waking can conclude this nightmare.'

Her runners keep discreetly quiet
For fear of engineering riot.
Captain Wright and Corporal Mercy
Count no stitches of her jersey.

The kids, now grown to stunted adults,
Look left and right for further insults.
A politician's black fur hat
Is doffed in tribute just for that.

Disgust conserve her guts in brine
Canned goods for these augustan lines.
Bits of here and there are scraped,
A sample bag (tagged and taped)
Interrogates the scientist:
Do these leavings from the cist
Indeed betoken Jean McConville
Broken on some devil's anvil?

Forensic science then commences
Poking for her mind or menses
Where the sands of time preserved
Things that left the boys unnerved.
Armed units of the DNA
Exhaust the twists and turns of play,
ad nauseam her guts in shingle,
Repeatly augustan jingle.

No country this for rhyme or treason,
Craft and crime both out of season.
(Neither prosecuted now
Were to do so mean a row.)
How to right it as it is?
How to write it as it is?
One line ends for Jean McConville,
Another start in Abbeyville.

SERMON ON THE MOUNTJOY SIDE-STEP

There is a bad smell in this pocket.
(Flann O'Brien)

1.

Abandoned
Responsible
The world is too late
For art, too soon
For justice.

Like Galileo's football
It lands on his feet.
The passes follow in poor play,
Suspects herded
Into the sport.

2.

Who made Granuaile?
I, said the Creator,
As paternal mater.
I made Granuaile.

My fault said Patrick.
With my shamrogue hat-trick,
I made Granuaile.

Shush, bellowed Cromwell.
Diverted from Hell
I made Granuaile.

Peace, murmured Swift.
Yet his style of thrift
Made Granuaile.

Strum, cried Wolfe Tone.
With my Jacobin jaw-bone
I made Granuaile.

My shout, claimed O'Connell.
Demagogic flannel
Made Granuaile.

Fellow sister! I'm Kitty.
My pelt was so pretty
It made Granuaile
Like wise Parnell.

   3.

Sir Roger Casement
(To his own amazement)
Laid Granuaile

And a new era dawned
As murderers fawned
To make Granuaile.

Lord Edward Carson
Whose protestant arson
Made Granuaile,

And the Boys of Kilmichael
Each on his 'cycle
Made Granuaile.

With John Charles McQuaid
Belt and crosier made
Poor Old Granuaile

While little Sean Russell
In his Nazi bustle
Made Granuaile.

Gerry Adams' guns
Out of public funds
Got knee-jerk reactions
From kids in traction

While provo and foe
Consubstantial did grow
To make Granuaile.

But their maker in tails
And immaculate shirt
From the Paris sales

Untaxed by Dirt,
Turned Grainne pale
When he didn't go to jail.

INCIDENT IN THE LIFE OF MICHAEL DAVITT
for Carla, his biographer

Governor Clifton bent over my notes as usual, reading as much as he could without seeming to seem he did, added his initials with a smirk of the pen.

Then it was time to talk with his prisoner a while. A friend – – had been excavating. An Egyptian mummy in a catacomb. No, not pharaonic, well not in the accepted or biblical sense. Yes, perhaps two thousand years, not much more. And a queen. The remains of a queen in whose hand the unnamed archaeologist found a few peas and some grains of wheat.

Softly clenched for a journey, as a child would clench sweeties.

Given two peas, my governor had sown them in his garden where they speedily took root and flourished. Next year he gives eight of the offspring to me. I plant them in 'my' walled garden where the only active foes are prowling snails.

And so, in a further year, I have secured a few hundred to take with me to Ireland, should I live to gain liberty, mummied here at a queen's pleasure, should I resume my journey.

This pea has a peculiar growth, being exceedingly slight in the stem just above ground, increasing in thickness upwards until, at six or seven feet, it becomes nearly as thick as a lady's wrist.

From a lost world, it comes to provender us a little. It bears a small white and pink flower, or rather two flowers of these colours. It is a large sized pea, and exceedingly fruitful. It requires constant watering.

*

Sunday 4 May 1884. Hail storm. Alas for my Portland seeds.

PELLETS OF STANZA AND PROSE

Found among ink cartridges
And a Bavarian coin
Of 1911
In a wooden signet-box
These too include metal work

Silver paper, picnic foil, shot
From the fowler's antique piece.
Some contain inanimate
Nature by way of snail-shell
And grit, with other roughage.

How to classify remains
Amongst which also canines
And less metaphorical
Bones – the stripped ribs and shoulders
Familiar after lunch, plus

Unassimilatable
Fur cast-offs – animal stuff
Never of other raptors:
In fairness, neither wisdom
Nor folly eats its own words.

At night when bats are flying abroad, they may be caught by owls.

Pellets from a great horned owl contained skulls of immature pallid bats. (After regurgitation these are easily taken for pat ballads.) It is a question for wise ones what dissection of their utterances might disgorge of prod and tague, red and trot yellow dog and yid.

NO SIGN GIVEN TO IT
          for Jean-Paul and Aideen Pittion

Once smelled of phosset.
The buyer of coffeegrinders,
Boxes of boxlike kitchen tools,
- Or beverage urns,
Braces of them (game for twins

He said, gone about the world)
Oldfashioned coffeegrinders
You could mincemeat in but
Throughout the gyres of their thick worms
Their coiled tongues

Were flecks of deadly fertilizer.
And we did nothing. But pace
The hardmongers' yard, measure
The bulk weight of opinion,
Resisting and lifting, face

Down the offer of action
And see in the mind's eye these things
Again now like unto stacked closed
Giants' eyelips
Or a midden of ragged bone.

Saw them a second time. And we did nothing?
Nothing better than measure
With broadest gesture of the arms
A distance between vagrant Minos
And his empty maze,

Between the here on the one hand
Writing and the other unraised.
        Yet twinned.
Blown about like wind.
Not much of a world.

Shoppers like him.
A few streets.
Fewer streets than out lasttime.
Fluttered remnants
Winnowed former innards.

                                ENVOI

                                The stop sign
                                Maculated
                                With virgin
                                Unbirth.

CLONALLIS, LATE SUMMER
for Mary FitzGerald

Between touching and the hours
A colossal vacancy,
Warren of souterrains.

The day repeated.
From a catalogue
The crest-laden

Tree knew not of
I would read
In my survival

How she makes art
As the results
Not an essence.

For example,
Out of
Not in, pain.

I nodded in the library
At the news,
Thumbed history.

Profound's nothing to say
Having done nothing but
Measured out a life.

From the guest-house,
A refugee bat
Was restored to the wood.

Elsewhere hands plunged
On the *cafetières*,
Demonstration models.

The real dogs us,
With like lack of truth we
Bow in prayer or shame.

15/08/02

NUTTING
for Conor Carville

1

Roses with hazel mix
In the garden
Where softest of hawthorns
Weather and harden,
The woods turn to porn.

When in the distant west
A man took the wrong part
In a local contest
Between tradition and the art
Of law, the bested

Just killed time till
His nineteen-year-old
Held her funeral
After the same tolled
Months of cancer.

Carried their answer
In cans to his orchard,
Poisoned his handsome
Trees while a church bell
Kept the family ransom.

Roses with hazel mix
In the garden
Where softest of hawthorns
Weather and harden,
The woods turn to porn.

2

South of somewhere
Else a tree saps itself
From iron scars
Driven in elfish
Malevolence.

Just one another
Among the anthromorphs;
Ash for sport perhaps,
Or the water-willow,
Never hostile.

    Adults
Congregate to hear
Confession. Their wish
Floods like a bog blister
Or like elm disease.

The forgotten
Natural disaster
Serves to nothing
Beyond the hollow
Stump for hallow.

Hidden fungus edges
Elizabethan ruff
On expelled cartridges,
The fowler's once
Innocent teeth.

No mind the layabout you
Or frenzied calculation;
No mind the rituals to come.

Under the hayshed
Bloodshed.

What won't he mention
Between the butchers' hook
And the British pension?
What counts for bounty
In the tortured county?

3

Our craft only irritates
The silence after an act.
Better had we other
Distractions, bar-food
Or messages, to offer.

Offerings far too small but
A goat nailed to the tree,
The go-between
Garden and gutter
Where all sounds failed,

The nut-brown viola
Laid aside in some one
Dear nook unvisited,
Relic of antic
Relict of none.

You will want before
I leave a sentence:
In place of blood ointment,
Instead of signals
Disappointment.

Were a single tree to rise up
From the punk
Spitting slugs or sucking
Its leaves back in place,
A single tree walking

And though spent fecund,
Intent on return
Like a sham prophet,
Not one of us would die
Once but a second.

THE BROKEN STILE

Ixion's wheel stood still in wonder.
                                                (Ovid)

1

What progress from hoe to daisy-cutter
In the manuals of pain
For one who shambles a new back-yard.

Among low hills of stony grey soil
Unmarked graves
Shallow gratitude to the gods

He stabs a boggy lawn
To learn the road a-right
Out of remote and dogged Hades.

*

Too long he strutted these woods
Rousing striped badger and sprite
With his discordant human paean

And – worse – turned aside to prate
Self-praise of the bard
And never endless song,

While his bridal goddess
Immortal and impatient
Paddled in water-cress

Gown up to broach the stream
Turning heads with a turn of the head
Engendering his dream.

2

Ere time there was before griefs.
A sufficiently small bang,
Indiscreet courtings, then

Driven to a clearing between trees
And dumped by the laughing females
Among countless dead birds.

He fumbled stubble and fallen jumps;
Seven ages passed
As he spun in the moonless dark.

At Cerberus' bark from a out-house
The hot pursuing headlamps
Swung down-hill undimmed.

His hands froze and melted.
His blood circled.
The spring leaves of his sweat

Opened, shone and sapped themselves.
Every forty-fold gash in his flesh
Mouthed her who made it.

3

Then he broke for cover
And simply fell over
A low rough-cut staircase

Of staves bound with tendrils,
Itself fallen
In the plantation,

An item of little more
Than past utility at best,
Debt of words, or just

An upturned triangle
Matted in sphagnum
Naked growth on dressed timber,

The strangest limb
Or thong he ever tasted
As he fell on it again.

4

Old growths of fern and moss
Cut and cured. The wooden
Trivet stood any ways,

Allusive to a fault,
Deserted alike among
Disappeared and unknowns.

The nearly dying
Hero denied himself anew:
The stile he leaned under

Upheld him erstwhile
The pursuers stagged off
To name the same game.

5

Near Magherafelt
Metaphor felt
Rarely important,

What a sister could not say
To her brother
Back from the sticks,

A mate of Orpheus
Who missed his end
Cutting his engine.

6

He away home across
Fields, counting
Beads of sweat

Welded to his palms,
Knowing only that
The iron ferry awaited.

7

Following and fleeing from themselves,
How many centuries of the hunt, the kill,
The undergrowth of remorse?

POMONA
after sculpture by Breon O'Casey

By late August the fruit is shed
With harsh winds blown side to side.
The new trees have settled,
Six water-fir rooting and blazing.
I know little of their language
Noting the few abrasions.

Impervious to mortal love,
Bravely facing into the earth,
You have fled so like the other fruit
Everything shuns with respect
The seat you occupied, as if
One of the disappeared had eaten it.

Take a simple lad in the high bog –
Hardly mountain, ungrazed
Hillside then and now a site for sites –
He yet eludes diggers that slog
At his recovery. Nightfall succeeds
Nightfall with hungry gaze.

The long acre darkens. We are invited
To watch TV news naked
With a presenter starkly unveiling
The day's atrocities and scoops.
In this universe of Us and the US,
Little foxes our mindlessness.

Of all that remains, the bronze of you
Alone resists annihilation,
Patiently waiting among cultivars

For the soil to open with frost,
Watching as only inanimate things may.
Who is to say between you and her?

Top-knotted, the back-view alert,
She only presents now you've gone
Down the nether lands, on descents
Where nothing means what I hear,
By falls of light stunned and overgrown;
And taken with you bough or basket.

Presents and looks away. An art
Of casting hands without suspicion
Of gestured surface appeal averts
The eye somewhere else before
It resumes to hug the lot, just as the eyes are
Just an outline of paired leaves.

Outside the fuel-bunker
An old crone keeps company or faith;
Keen winds ruffle a table-cloth
seriatim. The unseen one of us
Tramples tilth or filth, hunkered
Above the chopping-block.

Ixion's wheel

NEAR SIZEWELL BEACH
for J. H. D., 15 June 2002

Memory of the great sea is capacious.
An entire catchful of fish, or story
Of their pursuit and landing, tells little.

One hollow-tooth pebble shines from its nerve
Of captive water, a drop so small no
Shaking will dislodge it. Others dissolve.

We peer among the uncountable stones
And retrieve their mere namesake, gobbed aside
At someone's picnic near the White Lion.

Does the fruit-stone assume a shell
Exterior, protective of a self
Not knowable from the protection?

You walk ahead, your head introspective
Against the northern light, and point to sea.
One of the local craft is attempting

Landfall in circles of diesel and haze
To align itself between bodies of
Swimmers, early fall's playful survivors.

We stop, apart by a dozen paces,
Both this side of the elected beach-head.
The past you know clamps its hand on my face,

Something beyond our striving, outside time.
The fisherman takes the strain of a hawse
Tightening from his inshore winch. He makes

An angle of commemorated war,
Against the temple of an unclear power,
Its dome setting in the north, a *blanc* sun.

NOT YACHT-CLUB

Covered, uncovered, recovered
Beyond lough and togher
The impossible virgin lived
A hillside existence for one
Holy Helper dulling the pains
Of childbirth in others.

In legend or lyric
Fifty-eight churches were dedicated
To the sinster of her parish;
The prosaic, the Mosaic,
And downright perpendicular
All survived the iconoclasm.

Once at Villa Sacerdoti
– place too sure of itself –
Water under the statued shadow
Rose. May regatta of lost sails, light
Houses and dingy craft
Launch prayer to-or-for the wight!

Central to her cult is the miracle
Of swallowing by a sea-dragon
With his break-asunder to release her,
Whose bold comparison
Of Christ's bowels to the bowels of Hell
Was much quoted after.

Who made metals speak,
Restored the Prick of Conscience,
And interceded with Quintianus
The past prefect local people
Name Quinty for short

In her suffering absence?

At Combs and Strawless,
Doubtless obscured water,
She endures in stained grace:
Imperfection's best,
Both needle and anchor
— *her face, less clear and clearer.*

EURYDICE

The wild meadow
Rang to the stake.

She asked for love-music.
Two can't be alone.

Who could live enough
To sing her adequately?

What can I give
But words rescued

From the truth only
As we are from death?

   For the truth would render us up where the serpent rendered her down, should love rend us.

RHYMES FOR EURYDICE

I thought to build

    one singular guild

For retirement

    into remnant,

Grove of vanity

    with fern or foxglove,

And a bench for rest

    from all the rest.

Yet had I found

    no peculiar ground.

Whether

    by Grace concluded

From the motive race

    or by herbbush

And paradisal kerb.

Instead had bought

    a plainer plot

By Jim Clear's

    stock-car wilderness,

His Golgothan silent

    JCB

Penitent yet proud.

On the other side,

    let the raised head

Of Orpheus

    murmur this fuss

In the wax ear

    of his salvatrix.

THE GARDENS QUARTET

    i. *Saint Luke's Cross*

In front of a redstone quarry
We stood like youngsters
Facing the hippie's paradise.

For his open privacy
Showy artichokes
Burned blue at the top.

Brands of paraffin
Fought for our attention
As we gripped hands.

    ii. *Kylemore*

Your reverend cousin
Showed you all things
From her convent tower,

Beds laid out in whorls
Against the restored earth,
Their early autumn tones

Earmarked as if
Auriculas were
The one flower in the world.

iii. *Crawford*

Light glanced with envy
At your skin.
The air stood off.

Untold pictures
Shied to the skirting board
Away from your skirt:

No-one with a lute
Made trees
Abashed as these.

Under your handiwork
Bronze and wax flourish;
Copper pipes, and

Hardfern soothes the air
Flowerless and root-rich.
Your chosen cryptogam

Breeding in secret
Makes you the chosen
Mistress of your art
               And me.

iv. *Northern Landscape*

I missed you in Italy
On my walk in the woods.
The natural gallery

Led downwards
To a dry stream

The colour of your hair.

Only once have I escaped
From memory
Into the unshown:

Two birds rose
From your softest
Drumlins becoming
                My eyes.

Here too a place under
The living roots of fallen beech
Where we might.

UP AND UNDER

Of all the ladies
Confined to Hades
The lovely DJ
Eurydice
Was the peach.

She spun her discs
And ran some risks
Of innuendo
And out your other end – Oh
Let's not preach!

She longed for sighs
Between her thighs,
Her man expiring
While still desiring
Only her to teach.

My fructive maiden
Had music played on
Every frequency
While I'd seek and see
Her private breach!

Netting more nectar
Than Helen and Hector,
We rivaled bees
In honeysuckle trees
And the brazen beech.

She sipped at wine
Longing for mine;
In marbled halls

Toyed with balls
At my beseech.

Her bosom silk light
Was nearly milk-white
But for red nipples
Spurring dead cripples
To lust and leech.

She laughed at gags
And her favourite mags
Enjoying jokes
And amorous pokes
On our otherworld beach.

Betimes I died
On every tide
Toing and froing
Ebbing and flowing
Swooning and knowing
Coming and going
To foam and screech.

Above the gloom
Of Hades' bedroom
She eased burdens,
Released hard-ons
With enlightened speech.

Compared to the gods
I was long odds,
Yet she undid my skin
And slid her hand in
My soul to outreach.

Rescued like this
I went on the kiss
While she ate in turn
My face as it burned
Like a honey-glaze peach.

During her period
We were at it unwearied
By other passages
And nether massages
Pure Cupid would impeach.

Our spirited bodies
Drank sexual toddies
With bites for chasers
Eyes keen as lasers
Lest we underreach.

We polished the floor
With bum, back and shoulder.
No pale of exhaustion
Bold love was a caution
And night was our bleach.

We favoured the moon
To the blaze at noon:
We hogged the dark
And snogged in Cork
Each inside each.

On the Feast of Saint John
With no johnnie on,
We added one more
To our love-all score,
Legs all in a pleach.

Now you've conned these lines
On Eurydice's designs
And love of Orpheus
Whom she led from Chaos –
      Please don't peach!

ALLOTMENTS
school of Vallier

    i.

White snow
In the dark shade
Lights know
They made
If it were so.

    ii.

Dead growth
The gardener
Called it, loath
To pardon or
Condemn or both.

    iii.

See from the horizon
A tree being
Itself, neither
Beech nor evergreen,
Without kind.

Existence unattributable.

   iv.

The sleeper
Above the chimney,
Its shadow of ochre
Is neither art nor log.

   v.

The innocent
Dwell on befoulment,
The guilty pose
For questions of style.

   vi.

I remember
My grandfather's
Calloused fingers

Stiff knuckled,
And deadened
Finger tips.

His slater's knife
Terminated
fleur de lys.

What can I offer
But phrases of
Compared labour,

Little slab of
Effective grammar,
Handprinted stammer?

    vii.

Planting to rest,
Giving birth to waste,
Seated by the fire
Hat in place.

Preventable hope,
Packet of wild flower seed,
The messages.

    viii.

One sat
For Vallier
He or me or she

Artisan to
Artisan
Know it.

On cue
Off stage
The wingèd rival.

These?
The feathery strokes
Of his heels.

last thing

NUMBERS FOR JOSHUA AND ABIGAIL COHEN

    i.

There are fewer than you think.
Consider the acres of light
Which fell briefly.

Pistacchios and pitted olives –
It is a disgrace we agree
Leaning over the word
To open it anew.

    ii.

Somewhere there is a cave
Above buoyant deadness
Full of vestiges and shards
Drinking vessels of the spirit.

    iii. The Scribe

I have done much tonight
In the course of thirty minutes.
These things are rushed
To the detriment.

iv.

Forgive us o god
For gods sake
For our belief.

We mistake thy good
For our benefit.

For there is, but for us.
And there too
But not for us.

MISERERE

je suis seul – (Pascal)

Christ no more
Spent three days in Hell
Under American supervision
Than I do now
Expecting your answer.

Consider the facts.
He pegged it Friday
About three in the afternoon,
Was missing presumed
Alive by Sunday am.

That leaves forty-five hours
British Mean Time
Unaccounted,
And Hell in those reports
Was not even Greek

But a smoking place
The likes of which
We have forgotten
Our memories
And fulfilled plans of.

Why was it
Hope and
Expectation split?
Why Godot in Iraq
While God is good enough for us?

I too have seen
And not seen you
In the same twinkling,
Have hidden in bed
While things were settled.

The week-end creaks
With news bites
From the pottery,
Dopes in shackles
And a little child to lead them.

Listen to me, Boss.
I take the orders round here.
Badly, I admit, but gladly.
And get this,
Which I would not give.

You must judge
By freedom
If I am to dredge
Loathings
Off the page.

You might list
The human merits
I lack, writing
(If necessary) on
Both sides at once.

You may add vices
To make me blush
Though others
Keep me informed.
(Anger, I confess, endures.)

But guff me nothing
About Sacred and Profane
Waiting-rooms.
What love we hang on
We share among.

FOR BICE PORTINARI, FOR EXAMPLE

Every year I hear
My self blaspheme
Against the tongue
Set up to blast it.

Every month I hear
My self blaspheme
Against the tongue
Set up to blast it.

Every week I hear
My self blaspheme
Against the tongue
Set up to blast it.

Every day I hear
My self blaspheme
Against the tongue
Set up to blast it.

Every hour I hear
My self blaspheme
Against the tongue
Set up to blast it.

Every minute
Even second
Or moment
Blast blast it.

And anxious, O Lord,
How without hating
Hatred I disserve thee
Mating matrix

Of beauty with
Merest truth,
Merest, O Lord,
Making truth with

Each blastphoneme.
Hate this dedication
After three years.
Take it I deem

Take it I say
And stuff it, Lord,
Stuff it to thy bosom,
Against me.

MATIN
   of Wednesday 7 October 2001

If you had not left us
You could have prevented us.

                                                      Signs
                                                      are.

Now all we know
Is that you are

Mere substance
Mere word

Mere all.

If you had not prevented
So well

                                          We were not left here
                                          Between blown
                                          Husk and soil.

SALT AND LIGHT

The phone rings up
Some third anniversary
As if events did not stagger
Their order.

I need you
But you don't need me.
You may want me at times
But you don't need me.

You reach out of your goodness
And touch me for the first time
Again. For once.
And then again.

You call to me
Salt and light,
Diversely call me
To be salt and light.

You flummox me
Whom you made.
You wait
Passionately aside.

There was the beach,
The inland sea,
A ruined lodge.
Moments not scenes

I urge replies on you.
Or they fall through bare trees
Like snow, pre-papers really
Which have still to begin to grow.

I snatch back at one or two,
But will prefer
Threads of lavender
You need in prayer.

Catkins yet bigger.
Acorns but flat.
Scarves of thistledown.
Scrolled, purely interior bark.

One or two. Calling
And response;
Each absent from
The other   nearing

                                                    the timeless nondescript

ONE ANIMAL'S RETURN

> DOCTOR: 'Is your mind at ease?'
> GOLDSMITH: 'No, it is not.'

1

Dark scorpions on their bellies,
Proconsuls in wellies,
Rat will rhyme with swan
In their porno-infantry plan.

Attributes without substance,
Line obliterating lime.
Transcendent frightfulness,
So the books say little
Beyond outraged text
Laved with spittle
From slavish carcasses,
One lit by the next.

Mounds of refused flesh
Lay in mid-composition
Where the scribes drove in
After such knowledge in deed.
What sentence posed
Through bitsy time,
Even to say *Each together led
Their solitary way?*

2

'He was angry twice. My mother drove me back from Wicklow to Kenilworth Park, to tell how I had deliberately ruined the garden at Cronemore. With Jack I had run madly through it, again and again, bursting down rows of peas and beans, trampling cabbage plants and kicking open drills of potatoes. The garden was Granddad's preoccupation, where he brooded happily over his pipe, sitting under the ditch on a stool which wobbled to one side whenever he was not in place. He had won the garden out of a heavily screened field called The Paddock. Weeds had abounded there because it had been used years ago as a threshing yard, despite the upper section of apple trees, bristling gooseberry bushes – one encircled the most-easily climbed tree – and the remnants of a tennis court. I recall the wickedness in particular of kicking the drills open, the sudden release of energy as the foot came clear through the clay and rose with a fine brown spray, the effort to stay balanced for the next blow, and the next, as we zig-zagged up the drills, soiling the lower air with powdery bursts. My father took me upstairs to the front bedroom and beat me, not severely I have to say. Indeed perhaps less severely than he wanted my mother downstairs to believe. But then, there is a demand to remember well.'

3

That moment thou became he.
Knowing death found its tongue-
Tapped root, earth's first weed,
Cold male personality,

Unstable as water.
Words became things that are not,
After deliberate fire, after
And before. Conceived slaughter.

Swan with rat in unison:
Can tributes or substance
Act without penalties,
Corruption for precision?

> – Yet Hegel bought my drift in
> His forgotten *Frühe Schriften*;
> Ditto Yeats whose hate we hate
> And yea was nay beyond a doubt.

4

Vanity put aside
Bright as a wardrobe
Singeing its glad-rags
Whingeing sad rage,

So in worshipful fear
Stoking no mirrors of the soul
He impressed
Her fully small breast.

They broke, lapsing to traipse
Among creatures of their kind,
Riven from the nameless
Maker of all is said.

5

Mighty good
If God'ld
Direct my feet
To the funny side of the street

Though gutters
Splutter
Red Seas of blood
To my runny side of the meat.

Mistake my reference
For your reverence,
We oversweet
The honey side of my bleat.

Comic views,
Eternal news
Strong to sport
A sunny side of the truth.

6

When Judah traduced Tamar
Broken measures sung
Synchope, agape, dung
Of the master-stammerer.

Too strong an artifice
After the smoke has failed
To fall shapely or ladder lead
Deeper than smashed thighs.

Souls for gold fillings, cheap
Grace, new life in the Argentine.
A small business importing
Empty clothes. Christ,
Hang in there like a good man
And see us righted. The beast
Is gone with a few generations
Of shattering might and broken can.

7

Meaner and maker unspoken,
Devise no mega diva
Love governing her tent.
Our *via negativa*
Echoes without precedent –
'Master, thy word is past it.'
No way, uncreate, can bread
Resume as grain to die in bed.

NEARBY DRUNG, COUNTY CAVAN
For Jim and Louise
of Country and Western Research

Did failure
Spoil Jean Shepard,
Drive her
To Christ the Leopard
Among iron sheds
Like of these?

Did she hymn
Incognito
Between Drum
And Pettigo
In iron sheds
Like of these?

Corrugated
We called that.
And galvanized.
Rippled iron
Washboard
Blue-black as slate.

The nails too
Galvanized;
Four per sheet
Half-man-sized
On the strut,
Under sun or sleet.

We were not
Galvanized

Most of the week.
Feared not,
The rich would
Inherit the meek.

When we sang
We were nearer,
Never home.
Nearer rang
True as a nail
Bright as chrome.

A Good Shepherd
At the Tinahely Show
Struck out north
For Quinnsworth
When hailstones peppered
The bogs of Wicklow.

Yeats rang
No bells with us.
Butch more
Than Tom Moore.
We were the pits,
Not the pith.

Old William, you had
No eye
For the ordinary
Of this parish, these sheds,
Their ritual
With dry goods and fuel.

Socials, not dances.
Ethel, not Frances.

We were locked
In a security
You hocked
To glorify

A few gallons
Of land, former
Flax-pools, weavers
And winders, warmer
And steadier hearts to balance
Your chills and fevers.

For the record,
Jean married
Hawkshaw Haskins
Who died with Patsy Kline.
All white with the Lord,
Decent skins.

Old William, you sprang
From arm-strong
Seed hereabout
These iron sheds
You failed
To mention.

My Uncle Jock
Rose from Given's pit,
His lungs the like
Of rubber shreds
With asthma for chorus,
Under a Chrysler hearse

Warbled like a
Stabbed melodeon,

Rattled like a gear-box
Flying solo
For the Black Loughs
With every other swan.

Once inured
To its ironies
He too endured
The Patriot Game
At sing-songs
Or ding-dongs.

The galvanized echo
Of a sticky end:
In iron sheds
Like of these
A wake-widow cons
The People's Friend.

Jean caught the mood
At the funerals –
No 'Dear John' of course
But 'Heart, We Did
All That We Could'.

Could have been worse.

THE ENLIGHTENED CAVE

(composed 1983 in Washington,
in 2002 dedicated to Ilham Ibnou-Zahir)

-

(later the ice came)

grasses and herbs appeared
and birch and juniper were common

crouched skeleton with food
vessel in cist. The skull
and vessel empty.) [1]

•

cremated human bones in in-
verted urn, plus food vessel ²

•

pigmy cup found in a cist
grave with a crouched skeleton. ³

•

the blanketbogs of the higher mountains
started to grow enveloping the tombs and
farmsteads the terrible war which has just
ended gave rise to a great number of illnesses
of this kind

•

'wake
bageyed and erect'
or to be

forgetting
on the surface
blue, private, universal, open
the moist ring of heaven

•

Movius found here three unrolled implements. In the visible structure of the scientific treatise he leads his readers upward, chapter by systematic chapter, to the more sophisticated reaches of psychological analysis. In the invisible personal narrative he takes us downward, dream by dream, into the underground recesses of his own buried self.

•

not a hint of art
but creedview

not a hint of belief
but decoration

rude forefathers of
more and less

than

(below: two razor knives
the lower in the form
of a small fish.)

•

Clearly the open court was designed to accommodate the mourners at a funeral, it would hold about fifty people comfortably; indeed this court was paved near the entrance to the burial gallery, its sacred character emphasized by a polished diorite axehead at the entrance.

•

what happens to a name
it comes

to here aured by a chit of
profession

glinted and reduced
the thing if thing [4]

•

stonelined grave with cremated remains of a person about 30 (to left) covered by a flagstone on the underside of which there is ornament consisting of four groups of concentric circles. [5]

•

yes before.
A foil of ash over the surface.
Violet ash over the surface.
Extincture.
And the memory coyed
in near recovery
a commonwealth of grass and insects
genetic minutiae
signs
an altered rhythm here or change of order
a line of ash under the surface.

•

beforewe
orevenyou

before rhythm
and individuation

whole
who

(containing two small chisels,
a socketed knife with curved
blades and a socketed gouge

•

At the same time the freedom to experiment which their builders' economy enjoyed in placing the various elements of the tomb suggests they were built early in the tradition, too early for rigid academicism to have set in.

•

debitage the seas
maximum transgression
clearance the stands
oak and alder
radiocarbon estimates
a near thing
a material culture

•

return
return compulsion
disappearance and return
the tree Clorinda
I have returned to the stones.

gnomic psyche
whe?

nor Bran nor Flan
Only the mighty God

who changes not
even us

Notes: ¹ Keenoge ² Burgage ³ Drung ⁴ (Aughrim) ⁵ Ballinvalley

COLOPHON

take my breath

I am like a pelican of the wilderness:
I am like an owl of the desert.
I watch,
and am as a sparrow alone upon the housetop.
Mine enemies reproach me all the day;
And they that are mad against me
are sworn against me.
For I have eaten ashes like bread,
And mingled my drink with weeping.

Psalm 102

And I went unto the angel, and said
unto him, Give me the little book. And
he said unto me, Take it, and eat it up:
and it shall make thy belly bitter, but it
shall be in thy mouth sweet as honey.

Revelations,
Chapter 10.

www.ingramcontent.com/pod-product-compliance
Lightning Source LLC
Chambersburg PA
CBHW071729090426
42738CB00011B/2434